Happy Birthday Me

A Comedy

Simon Williams

A SAMUEL FRENCH ACTING EDITION

FOUNDED 1830

SAMUELFRENCH-LONDON.CO.UK
SAMUELFRENCH.COM

CHARACTERS

Margot Buchanan, an actress
Miss Freda Deacon, an elderly actress
Mrs Kidd, the home administrator
Sir Leo Buchanan, an actor
Lady Buchanan, Leo's wife
Sadie Croft, a young actress
Superman, an unwelcome visitor
Graham Latimer (voice off)

The action takes place in the lounge of an actors' retirement home on the South coast

Time—the present

Other plays by Simon Williams published by
Samuel French:

Double Death
Laying the Ghost
Kiss of Death
Nobody's Fool
Nobody's Perfect

HAPPY BIRTHDAY ME

The lounge of an actors' retirement home on the South coast

A mobile phone is ringing as the CURTAIN *rises*

Freda, an eccentric elderly resident, takes off her iPod and answers it

During the following speech, Mrs Kidd, the home's administrator, enters. She is holding a newspaper

Freda Hallo. This is Margot Buchanan's phone ... No, I'm someone else — never mind who ... A fellow resident, I'm in the room next door to hers ... Is that who I think it is? ... Aha, well, she doesn't want to speak to you ... We both don't. Because you're unspeakable and so are your films.

Mrs Kidd Good morning, Miss Deacon.

Freda (*hanging up hurriedly*) Morning, Matron.

Mrs Kidd So who was that?

Freda It was a wrong number, for Margot.

Mrs Kidd Is that right, Miss Deacon?

Freda Margot does not need to be harassed on her birthday, and not by that ocean-going twat.

Mrs Kidd You don't mean Sir Leo?

Freda I do. There's no point in trying to be pally with your exes, I say. I hated all mine.

Mrs Kidd (*opening her newspaper*) All over the front of the *Daily Mail*. Drunk as a lord apparently.

Freda (*studying the paper*) It used to be two fingers for a V-sign. Is this new one fingered thing European, do you suppose?

Mrs Kidd Well, I don't want Mrs Buchanan seeing it.

Freda If she does, we'd better take to the hills. When she heard he'd sold the Augustus John painting, she didn't speak for three days, not even to her bookmaker.

Mrs Kidd It touched a nerve. He can't need the money, surely.

Freda It's of her after all. It was a wedding present from her to him.

Mrs Kidd (*picking up and rattling a small money box*) Her swear box is nearly full as it is. I can't be charging enough.

Freda One pound for the F-word is a bit steep, but ten pence a pop for the odd "bugger" is a bargain. Happy birthday, darling.

Margot enters

Margot I could kill you, Freda. You've told everyone. There'll be cakes and speeches and God knows what. Ronnie Machin says he's arranged a kissogram from Hove.

Mrs Kidd It's all right, Mrs Buchanan, I'll make him cancel it.

Margot Good. He's an unspeakable little nerd. Am I allowed nerd, Mrs Kidd?

Mrs Kidd As it's your birthday.

Margot Just as a matter of interest, how stupid does everyone around here think I am?

Freda Compared to whom, my darling?

Margot All over the building, every single copy of the *Daily Mail* seems to have gone into auto-destruct. Apparently copies have been lost, damaged, defaced, burnt and even vomited on. (*Beat*) Did Arsenal lose again last night? Or — could it be dear old Leo?

Freda Of course it's Leo.

Mrs Kidd Is he dead?

Freda No.

Margot Don't tell me he's won an Oscar.

Freda (*showing her the paper*) There.

Margot (*peering*) Oh my God ... Is that his finger in the foreground?

Freda Yes. It's a kind of one-legged V-sign.

Margot Read me what it says.

Freda (*reading*) "*The Sheriff of the Universe* star, Sir Leo Buchanan, responded angrily to rumours about his personal life last night. He swung a punch at a journalist from a Sunday newspaper."

Margot *Cherchez la femme* again, is it?

Freda "Hunt the bimbo," it says here.

Mrs Kidd (*taking back the paper*) On page five, there's a picture of his wife. "Lady Buchanan stands by her man."

Margot I bet she does the ——— . How much for bitch?

The telephone rings. Margot answers it

(*Into the telephone*) Hallo ... Yes?

Freda Put it on speaker ...

Margot puts it on speaker

Graham Latimer (*off*) Hallo. Is that Margot Buchanan?

Margot Maybe.

Graham Latimer (*off*) It's Graham Latimer here. I'm with the *News of the World*. As Sir Leo's first wife, I wondered if you felt ——

Margot Are you the one he bopped last night?

Graham Latimer (*off*) Yes.

Margot No comment.

Graham Latimer (*off*) Is that all?

Margot How about — no comment, scumbag. (*She hangs up*)

Mrs Kidd By the way, your visitor has arrived, Mrs Buchanan, she's waiting in my office.

Margot Visitor. What visitor?

Mrs Kidd Miss Sadie Croft. Actress — going to play Juliet. I'll fetch her.

Margot (*recalling*) Bugger. Bugger. Bugger.

Mrs Kidd That's rather extravagant, Mrs B.

Margot puts coins in the money box

Margot Bugger. Bugger. Bugger. (*She puts in three more coins*) I
thought I'd put her off. Bound to be grungy.
Mrs Kidd I'd better bring you another pile of ten pence coins while
I'm about it ...

Mrs Kidd exits

The telephone rings. It's still on speaker

Margot (*answering*) This is a recorded message. Please speak after
the bleep. Bleeeeeep.
Sir Leo (*off*) Happy birthday. It's me. Leo. I just spoke to some old
crone who said you wouldn't speak to me.
Margot (*into the telephone*) BOG OFF, LEO. (*Hanging up*) You
weren't going to tell me?
Freda I thought you had enough on your plate with the kissogram.
Margot Thanks. (*A beat*) Funny, isn't it? I only have to hear his voice
or see his picture and all the old symptoms come right back, the
irritation, the nausea, the sense of foreboding.

Sadie Croft enters. She overhears this last line

Sadie Not about me I hope ...
Margot Ah, you must be ...
Sadie Sadie Croft.
Margot Of course. This is Freda Deacon.
Sadie Not *the* Freda Deacon?
Freda No — probably another one. It's Margot's birthday. Seventy.
Sadie Many happy returns. Actually I'm amazed you didn't cancel.
You must get swamped with grungy young drama students.
Margot Good Lord, no. I've been looking forward to it, haven't I,
Freda?
Freda Oh yes.
Margot I'm not sure I'll be any use to you. It's over forty years since
I played Juliet.
Sadie Forty-three. With Leo Buchanan as your Romeo.

Freda Yuk. Yuk. Yuk.
Margot Headphones, Freda. Put them on.

Freda puts on her headphones. She dances then sits

Sadie In his biography P.J. Monkton says the emotional heat between the two of you on the first night was palpable.
Margot He was a very discerning critic. A lot of water has flowed under the bridge.
Sadie You haven't changed a bit. You look so ——
Margot — well preserved. Don't say it.
Sadie I was at Sotheby's last month when they auctioned the Augustus John — the one of you in the rose garden.
Margot (*curious*) Were you?
Sadie Yes ... You weren't tempted to put in a bid?
Margot No ... At eighty-five thousand pounds. To hell with it.
Sadie I loved it. You looked so invincible.
Margot Invincible. Yeah. Well, that was then ... So ...
(*As Juliet*) "I have bought the mansion of love,
                But not possessed it ..."
Don't you love that line? Go on. From there ...
Sadie (*as Juliet*) " ... and though I am sold,
                Not yet enjoyed; so tedious is this day
                As in the night before some festival
                To an impatient child that hath new robes
                And may not wear them ..."
Margot Very nice.
Sadie Shall I go on?
Margot No. Please don't. I know how it ends. The thing is to keep it simple. Juliet is simple, isn't she? Straightforward. She's naturally happy, don't you think? That's what makes her tragic.
Sadie Yes.
Margot Always look for the contrast. That's what all art is. Find the contrast — the conflict inside. Light against dark. Quick after slow. Happy then tragic. It gives you a journey.
Sadie (*writing*) "... find the conflict ..."

Margot Don't write it down. We always remember advice if it's any good.

Sadie What else?

Margot Let me see. Always have more breath than you think you need. New breath for a new thought. In-spir-ation.

Sadie (*taking note*) That's very good.

Margot It's just technique. (*Studying Sadie*) Don't scowl. Juliet doesn't scowl and neither should you. Juliet has her eyebrows up. As a general rule: eyebrows up for innocence and hope. (*Demonstrating*) Down for puzzlement and anger. See?

Sadie Yeah. That's cool. What about the "palpable heat"?

Margot Well, that's something else, isn't it? Do you have a boyfriend?

Sadie Sort of.

Margot Hm. Was it him who gave you that scent? The *Ysatis*?

Sadie Yes.

Margot I see ... Love is a kind of recognition, isn't it? Recognition of who you are.

Sadie Is that what made for the "palpable heat" between you and Sir Leo?

Margot I think that was more hormonal.

Sadie It says in the book that his leaving you broke your heart.

Margot Leo didn't leave me, I threw him out. And I had a dodgy heart anyway.

Sadie It can't have been easy.

Margot Compared to giving up smoking it was a cinch.

Sadie The show must go on and all that?

Margot Crap cliché. Why must it go on? The theatre doesn't heal old wounds, you know, it seeks them out and rubs salt in them.

Sadie You're not in touch with him then?

Margot Nope. (*Flaring up*) Look of all the topics of conversation on God's earth, Leo Buchanan is the one I'd ... least ...

Sadie I'm sorry — I didn't realize.

Margot What didn't you realize?

Sadie Nothing. Sorry.

There is a moment between them

Mrs Kidd enters

Mrs Kidd Lady Buchanan is here to see you, Mrs Buchanan.
Margot Lady Buchanan. Is this a joke?
Mrs Kidd No.
Margot I thought you said you had cancelled the kissogram.
Mrs Kidd Shall I bring her in?
Margot Oh bollocks.
Mrs Kidd That'll cost you twenty pence, Mrs B.
Margot Twenty?
Mrs Kidd They come in pairs. Ten pence each.

Margot puts coins into the tin

Lady Buchanan enters

Lady Buchanan I thought if I rang ahead, you'd probably say
   you were busy, so I decided I'd just come by and say hallo — or
   something.
Margot (*cold as ice*) Or something.
Lady Buchanan And happy birthday, of course.
Freda (*taking off her earphones*) Oh. Hallo. Are they putting you in
   Nora Ramone's old room?
Lady Buchanan Good Lord, I'm not here as a resident, thank you
   very much.
Mrs Kidd Would you like a coffee, Lady Buchanan?
Lady Buchanan Thank you.
Margot I'd like a brandy.
Lady Buchanan Make it two.
Freda Three.
Mrs Kidd Any advance on three?
Sadie No, thank you.

Mrs Kidd exits

Freda puts her headphones back on

Margot I'm so sorry — this is Sadie Croft — Lady Buchanan. She's going to play Juliet.

Lady Buchanan Lovely. I remember seeing my husband ... Oh Christ.

Margot Lady Buchanan was going to say she remembers seeing Sir Leo and me in the nineteen sixty-eight production when she was five.

Lady Buchanan I hadn't imagined putting my foot in it quite so badly or quite so soon. Good luck with it.

Sadie Thanks. Perhaps I think I'll just go and er ... make a phone call ...

Sadie exits

Pause. Margot takes her pulse

Lady Buchanan What are you doing?

Margot Checking my pulse. I have a bad heart. It doesn't like surprises.

Lady Buchanan Neither do I.

Margot Or Marmite. I can't quite fathom why you should drive all the way down here from Chalfont St Giles just to wish me a happy birthday.

Lady Buchanan I brought you a card. It may relieve your curiosity.

Margot (*taking it*) Surely you could have sent it, Lady Buchanan?

Lady Buchanan There's no point in asking you to call me Judy?

Margot Absolutely not. (*She throws the card in a waste-paper basket*)

Lady Buchanan My, oh, my ... It's Chalfont St Peter, by the way, not Giles. You're right of course it's just a pretext.

Margot For what?

Lady Buchanan It's been a long time since we first met.

Margot Thirty-three years.

Lady Buchanan It's still etched in my memory. Isn't it time to bury the hatchet, Margot, to end your disdain for me, your dislike — your hatred, call it what you will.

Margot Hatred is fine with me. You say it's etched in your memory.

Lady Buchanan In every detail.

Margot Mine too. May the twelfth, nineteen seventy-eight. This is when I walked in and found you *in flagrante* with Leo.

Lady Buchanan Sort of ...

Margot Sort of? Did my eyes deceive me?

Lady Buchanan No ... What I meant was ...

Margot What?

Lady Buchanan We'd actually finished.

Margot Finished?

Lady Buchanan The *flagrante* thing ...

Margot Oh, well, that makes all the difference. (*Pause*) Leo was smoking a *Gauloise*.

Lady Buchanan He's given up now, thank God. You said you hoped I'd rot in stinking putrefaction.

Margot Not all wishes come true. (*She checks her pulse*)

Lady Buchanan I do get athlete's foot from time to time, if that's any comfort. How's your pulse?

Margot It's fine. Um ... look — you may find this hard to believe, Lady Buchanan, but I actually dislike you in your own right. I know you've got many wonderful qualities — I've read about them in *Hello* magazine. You want me to stop hating you, I can't. I've grown accustomed to it the way an old house gets used to the ivy.

Lady Buchanan You say it has nothing to do with Leo.

Margot Not a bit, you're welcome to him.

Lady Buchanan You always thought he'd come back.

Margot I wouldn't have him. He's gone off anyway.

Lady Buchanan What do you mean?

Margot Those new teeth for a start. He's gone downhill.

Lady Buchanan His knighthood counts for nothing then?

Margot Not a scintilla ... It's like giving an old car an MOT these days.

Lady Buchanan He's one of our great actors.

Margot No, he damn well isn't. *The Sheriff of the Universe* is not great acting, it's sheer greed. Oafish, nauseating greed.

Lady Buchanan You really are quite cantankerous, aren't you?

Margot I'm doing my level best.

Lady Buchanan And you can honestly say that it has nothing to do with the selling of the Augustus John.

Margot is ice cold

Margot (*with restraint*) Go away, Lady Buchanan. Leave me alone.

Lady Buchanan It was Leo's painting.

Margot It was my face, my dress. My father's rose garden. I paid for it.

Lady Buchanan It was a present.

Margot From me to Leo. Look — I don't want to talk about it. Not to you or anybody. Go back to Chalfont St bloody Peter.

Lady Buchanan There's something I'd like to say ...

Margot The subject is closed.

Lady Buchanan So the ivy gets no right of reply?

Margot's telephone rings. She answers it. The speaker is off

Margot (*into the telephone, discombobulated*) Hallo ... Yes ... No ... Goodbye ... Wait ... (*In a quandary; calling to Freda*) Freda ... Freda ... Will you take Lady Buchanan to the bar, please. Now.

Freda (*taking off her headphones*) Oh. Right. Er ... (*To Lady Buchanan*) Come with me, will you? Have you ever had a Saga Slinger, dear? It's a cocktail I invented — mostly gin.

They exit

Margot (*into the telephone*) Hallo, Leo... Yes. Where the hell are you? ... What conservatory? ... What do you mean behind ——

Sir Leo enters furtively behind her. He is wearing dark glasses and a muffler hides his lower face. He is speaking on his mobile phone

(*Seeing him*) — me. Oh, my God.

Sir Leo (*on his mobile*) I came to wish you happy birthday.

Margot (*into telephone*) Go away.

Sir Leo (*on his mobile*) Do you think we should hang up?

Margot (*into telephone*) Yes. Goodbye.

They both hang up

Is this you incognito?

Sir Leo Yes, I'm on the run from the paparazzi — incognito. I'll take them off. (*He takes his glasses off*) There.

Margot Aren't you rather old to go hitting reporters?

Sir Leo It's all right — he was quite small. I'm in a bit of a mess.

Margot Never! Go away. Bog off.

Sir Leo You're cross. Of course you're cross. I'd be cross if I turned up here without warning me. (*Pause*)

Margot is sulking

Seventy, eh? You look terrific. Lovely. (*Pause*) "But soft, what light through yonder window breaks..." (*Pause*) It's not bad here. Light. Cosy. (*Pause*) Margot, I haven't got time for you to go through a full scale sulk, can't we fast forward to the monosyllabics. (*Pause*) Actually I was frightened you'd throw something, a vase or a fit, because of ... the Augustus John.

Margot looks at him in silent anger

It's been sold. Auctioned. Did you know? (*Pause*) You're upset?... You don't give a damn? ... Tick one of the above.

Margot (*quietly*) Go away. Go away, Leo.

Sir Leo That's the "upset" box, right?

Margot Leave me alone and take your beastly wife with you.

Sir Leo My beastly wife ... My wife ... What do you mean ... my wife?

Margot Your spouse. Your consort. Your other half.

Sir Leo Judy.

Margot That's the one. She's in the bar with Freda Deacon.

Sir Leo What is she doing here?

Margot She said she'd come to make peace.

Sir Leo Peace. Christ. Judy doesn't make peace. Must have been a shock for you. You haven't seen her since ...

Margot Nineteen seventy-eight. She looks better with her clothes on.

Sir Leo What did you talk about?

Margot You know, this and that. What you were like in bed.

Sir Leo Did you? I mean you didn't ... What else?

Margot Your new teeth.

Sir Leo My teeth?

Margot She seemed to think they came with your knighthood. Go home, Leo. It's my birthday and the last thing I need is you turning up after all these years disguised as Jack Nicholson.

Sir Leo You're loving every minute of it.

Margot Not one jot. Why should I have to put up with the shambolic pile of crap that passes for your life being dumped in my lap? The mystery, the intrigue, the paparazzi and that maddening ghastly woman, your wife. You are a nightmare, Leo, as always, you are an appalling man — vain, cowardly, duplicitous, callow and what's the other one they use for politicians?

Sir Leo Sleazy.

Margot Exactly. Very, very sleazy.

Sir Leo Bravo. I'd forgotten how ludicrous you get when you're cross, my darling. All pompous and high blown and sexy as hell.

Margot You are an abomination. And don't call me that.

Sir Leo You know what's happened to you. You've got old.

Margot (*her dander up*) That's what happens to people with the passage of time. Some of us manage it with a little dignity.

Sir Leo   "Nay, sit, good cousin Capulet;
                 For you and I are past our dancing days."

Margot Clear off. Leave me alone.

Sir Leo What's wrong with my teeth anyway?

Margot They just need running in a bit.

Sir Leo You don't like them?

Margot I am supremely indifferent to them. You've stopped smiling that's all. All those terrible films.

Sir Leo The Sheriff of the Universe is always smiling. (*Acting it*)
"Defend the galaxy with pride, kiddo."
Margot You look like a cross between Bugs Bunny and Ken Dodd.

Sir Leo laughs. A moment between them

Sir Leo I can't believe you're seventy. You do look magnificent.
Margot Magnificent is the word for a mountain range or a battleship.
Sir Leo Exactly.
Margot Bastard.
Sir Leo You know, at the end of the day we are two of a kind.
Margot There's no need to be rude.
Sir Leo Sometimes I think to hell with it, all the Hollywood crap —
the hype, the salads, the bullshit ... the whole wretched rigmarole.
All I really want is to be sitting on a terrace in the South of France
with a great wall of bougainvillea behind me, a glass of Pouilly
Fuissé in front of me and you beside me playing backgammon in
a dotty old hat.
Margot (*warmly*) You are so full of shit.
Sir Leo Why would I lie?
Margot You always liked to keep in practice.

Sadie enters

Sadie I hope I'm not interrupting.
Margot Not at all. Sadie, this is Leo Buchanan — Sadie Croft.
Sir Leo How do you do?
Sadie How do you do? I'm so thrilled to meet you.
Sir Leo Thank you.
Margot Sadie is going to play Juliet.
Sir Leo Ah. Good. Lovely.
Margot She's been reading P.J. Monckton's book.
Sir Leo (*quite nervy*) He's just a poncy old windbag with his head up
his arse. Margot was the best Juliet ever.
Sadie That's why I came to see her.

Sir Leo I see. Well, the great thing is always to have more breath ...
Margot She knows already.
Sir Leo Well — good luck with it.
Sadie Thank you. Yes.

A tricky pause

Margot So, Miss Sadie Croft, how long has this been going on?
Sadie What do you mean?
Sir Leo She knows.
Sadie What do you mean? What does she know?
Margot I know the boundaries of coincidence. I know you're wearing *Ysatis* which is Leo's favourite scent. I see you have an aquamarine ring just like mine, and I know what a sucker I've been.
Sir Leo I am so sorry.
Margot I don't like being taken for an idiot.
Sir Leo It's not how it looks, I promise.
Margot Don't do that, don't promise, Leo. It always means you're lying.
Sadie You must think I'm a right cow coming here.
Margot Yup, that pretty much covers it. It's a bit of a Groundhog Day for me — the last time he was caught cheating on his wife I was in the title role. Are you really playing Juliet?
Sadie Yes.
Margot You don't think you might have mentioned that you were in fact shacked up with the Sheriff of the Universe here?
Sadie Actually I very nearly did.
Sir Leo I don't care for "shacked up with".
Sadie We're in love.
Margot Aaah.
Sir Leo More or less. We have an understanding.
Margot And that poor daft creature through there in the bar, your wife, doesn't know about this?
Sir Leo Not really ... not yet.
Margot She has no understanding of your understanding?

Sadie You haven't told her?

Sir Leo I haven't had a chance.

Sadie (*flaring up*) You said it was all over between you, Leo. That things hadn't been right for ages.

Sir Leo They haven't. She just hasn't noticed. She's been very busy with the new kitchen and things. It needs delicate handling.

Margot Reading about it in the *News of the World* should help soften the blow.

Sir Leo Please, Margot. We don't need your snide little jokes.

Sadie You said you were going to have it out with her, get it out in the open.

Sir Leo I am. I will. She's not one of those "let's-sit-and-talk-this-through" kind of people.

Margot More of a "rolling-pin" kind of person.

Sir Leo Margot, please. Sadie, I'm under a lot of pressure. Be patient.

Sadie To hell with this. I'm going to talk to that *News of the World* guy out on the lawn ...

Sir Leo No. Let's all stay calm ...

Lady Buchanan enters

Lady Buchanan Ah, there you ——

Sir Leo Hi. Yes, here I am.

Margot There he is indeed. Bingo. I think that gives me a full house.

Sir Leo Just popped in to wish Margot happy birthday.

Lady Buchanan Did you? Very nice too. (*To Sadie*) Bit of a bonus for you, eh?

Sadie I beg your pardon?

Lady Buchanan Leo played Romeo, didn't you, Leo?

Sir Leo Yes ... Long time ago.

Lady Buchanan He's always been keen on giving young aspirants a helping hand.

Sadie Is that right?

Sir Leo I do what I can.

Sadie (*threateningly*) We were discussing how to achieve "the palpable heat"?

Margot It can be so elusive...

Lady Buchanan Darling, we'd better be off. He's exhausted. He's been rather over doing it, haven't you my pet?

Sadie Burning his candle at both ends? That can be such a mistake.

Margot Especially if it's a rather short candle.

Freda enters. She is wearing her iPod

Freda (*shouting*) Is this the surprise party?

Margot (*loudly*) iPod, darling, take it off.

Freda (*taking it off*) Sorry ... Pink Floyd. Is everything all right?

Margot I'm doing an episode of "I'm a Celebrity Get Me Out of Here".

Lady Buchanan Freda, have you met my husband?

Freda No, I don't think so, but you never know, do you?

Lady Buchanan Sir Leo Buchanan.

Freda Freda Deacon. How do you do?

Sir Leo How do you do?

They shake hands

Freda Are you moving in here?

Lady Buchanan He's a film star for goodness' sake.

Freda Never mind. That won't worry them. We even had an agent in here once.

There is a silence. Freda puts her iPod back on

Sir Leo Come on, Judy, we'd best be going.

Sadie Not so fast. (*To Lady Buchanan; with menace*) Aren't you curious about what's going on here, Lady Buchanan?

Lady Buchanan Not especially.

Sir Leo Tell you what ... er ... Sadie, I'll give you a call some time and we could maybe do some work on your Juliet, hm? How about that?

Sadie Bollocks to that. Tell her.
Lady Buchanan Tell me what?
Sir Leo Nothing.
Margot Tell her, for God's sake.
Sir Leo Shut up, Margot. It's none of your business.
Margot (*shouting*) It's my birthday. All I wanted was a bottle of Claret and a couple of winners at Sandown.
Sadie Tell her, Leo.
Sir Leo It's not the time or the place ...
Sadie *News of the World*, Leo. Graham Latimer is out on the lawn.
Lady Buchanan What is all this about?
Sadie It's about us.
Lady Buchanan Us? You and my husband?
Sadie Yes. That's it.
Lady Buchanan Leo, what is she saying? Tell me she's not telling me there's something going on between the two of you.
Sir Leo I can't.
Lady Buchanan You can't what?
Sir Leo I can't tell you she's not telling you that.
Lady Buchanan You mean you've been having an affair with this girl?
Sir Leo Yes.
Lady Buchanan Behind my back?
Sir Leo Yes.
Lady Buchanan Is this true?
Sadie Yes.
Lady Buchanan I don't believe it. Under my nose?
Margot Hang on. You can't have it both ways.
Lady Buchanan What?
Margot It can't be behind your back and under your nose.
Lady Buchanan Shut up.

Sir Leo's mobile rings

Sir Leo (*answering it*) Hallo ... Yes. Ah ... Graham. How's the ...?
Is it? ... Try putting a raw steak on it ... Well, we're just having

a bit of a birthday party. A few laughs, you know. My wife and I'll pop out later for a few pics. OK? ... Cheers. Bye ... (*Hanging up*) Now perhaps we should all sit down calmly.

Lady Buchanan I'm not bloody well sitting down calmly.

Sir Leo It's all over, I tell you ...

Sadie You bastard.

Sir Leo Judy, it's all a storm in a teacup.

Lady Buchanan You bastard.

Freda (*taking the iPod off*) ... Bastard? What bastard?

Margot Shush, Freda. This bastard.

Sir Leo Margot ...

Margot No, we're unanimous.

Sir Leo What?

Margot You are a bastard. Always were.

Sir Leo No ... I am not really ... a bastard ... (*He lets out a huge groan of pain and falls to the floor*)

Lady Buchanan Leo. Leo, what are you playing at?

Sadie He's fainted.

Lady Buchanan Put his head between his knees.

Margot He's having a heart attack.

Lady Buchanan Oh, my God. Not now. Loosen his tie.

Freda Is he drunk?

Margot Quiet, Freda. Get Mrs Kidd ...

Lady Buchanan Somebody call an ambulance. (*To Leo on the floor*) It's all right my darling, I'm here.

Margot Yes. We all are.

Superman enters through the window. Chaos from now on. His English is not good

Superman Hi. Me Superman. I come for to kiss Mrs Buchanan. Superman kisses big. He kisses wet. Happy birthday — which one?

Lady Buchanan Get him out of here?

Margot Go away.

Superman I must kiss.

Margot You are not wanted.
Freda I wouldn't mind.

Mrs Kidd enters

Mrs Kidd What is all this noise? Oh, my ... (*Seeing the body*)
Ah ... stand back, everybody. Let's see what we've got here. (*To
Superman*) You. Out. Go. Shoo ...
Freda (*shouting*) You go back to Gotham city.

Mrs Kidd is busy with Sir Leo. Lady Buchanan is there too

Margot Clear off. You are not wanted. (*To Freda*) Superman is
actually from Krypton.
Superman I come from Littlehampton. I have docket for kissing.

Sir Leo lets out a deathly gasp

Mrs Kidd I'm not getting a pulse ... (*To the body*) Sir Leo ... (*Giving
resuscitation*) Sir Leo ... (*A thump*)

Pause

Lady Buchanan Anything ...?
Mrs Kidd I'm afraid not.

They all mutter their distress

Lady Buchanan Oh, no ... Oh, no ... Do it again. Give him another
thump. Keep trying.

*The resuscitation continues. The dialogue overlaps. Superman looks
on*

Superman (*recognizing Sir Leo*) Hey ... That's Sheriff of Universe.
All Ssssssh ...

Mrs Kidd I'm not getting a pulse ... I'm afraid ... there's no use. He's
    gone ...
Superman Defend the galaxy with pride.
Lady Buchanan Dead ... He can't be ... Leo ... Leo ...

CURTAIN

SCENE 2

An hour later. It is raining

*They are all sitting in disbelief. Each with a Kleenex. Mrs Kidd is
collecting the used tissues in a waste-paper basket from each of
them in turn*

Lady Buchanan So ... where will they take him for the post-
    mortem?
Mrs Kidd Worthing Hospital. They're very good there.
Lady Buchanan I just can't believe it. Just like that ... He wasn't that
    old. Sixty-eight.
Margot Seventy-one.
Lady Buchanan Sixty-eighty in his passport.
Margot Maybe, but seventy-one on his birth certificate. They made
    him lop three years off when he was a child star in the forties, and
    then when he got his scholarship to RADA, he sort of forgot to put
    them back.
Sadie He told me he was fifty-nine.
Lady Buchanan You keep your nose out of this. (*Pause*) He was a
    dear man. A dear ... dear man.
Margot Yes, he was. In his way. A dear man.
Sadie Yes, he was a ... Sorry.
Freda I never liked him.
Margot You didn't know him, for God's sake.
Freda Oh, didn't I? We did *Good Companions* in Weston-super-
    Mare once.

Margot What ...?
Freda He'd forgotten of course. (*Wistfully*) It was the year Devon
Loch won the Derby.
Margot (*flustered*) Freda — go to the bar. Pink Floyd — pink gin.
Go.

Freda exits

She's a bit soft round the edges at times.
Sadie They didn't. They can't have ... I mean did she mean ...?
Margot No, she didn't.
Lady Buchanan (*weeping softly*) Oh, my poor Leo. He was never
very good at handling stress.
Margot God knows he created enough of it.

Margot's mobile rings

(*Into telephone*) Hallo ... Graham, this is not a good moment... Yes,
we're all here ... No ... Sir Leo is ... He's not available at the moment
... Hm?

Mrs Kidd goes to the window. She can see Graham

The ambulance was for Superman. His back was in spasm ... Sadie
Croft? ... Yes ... I'll tell her ... Yes. You wait there ... Haven't you
got an umbrella? ... Oh, well. Tough shit. (*Hanging up and putting
money in her box*) Ten p for shit, is it? (*To Sadie*) He wants to talk
to you.
Sadie Oh, does he?
Mrs Kidd I'll have him removed. Perhaps you'd like to come and
wait in my office, Lady Buchanan?

Mrs Kidd exits

Lady Buchanan I don't want to seem vindictive, Miss ...
Sadie Croft.

Lady Buchanan Miss Croft. I don't know what your relationship was
with my husband. I don't want to know. I never want to see or hear
from you again, not in the press, not through solicitors, not at all. Do
I make myself clear?

Sadie Perfectly ... I didn't want to fall in love with him, you know.

Margot None of us did.

Sadie I actually felt for you, Lady Buchanan, as one woman to
another.

Lady Buchanan I wasn't looking for sistership, Miss Croft.

Lady Buchanan exits

Pause

Margot Poor you. (*Giving Sadie a brandy*) It's never been much of a
part, "the other woman".

Sadie Not one to get type-cast in. Are you all right?

Margot Not altogether.

Sadie Me neither. I'm very sorry I deceived you. I hope you're not
cross or jealous or whatever?

Margot With you? Not really. Well, only a bit. I mean if someone
crashes your car that's upsetting but if you sell it to someone and then
he crashes it, it's not quite so bad. (*Toasting*) To Leo.

Sadie To Leo.

Margot (*reflectively*) I remember the first time I saw him. The first
rehearsal for *Romeo and Juliet*, at the stage door of the Globe. He
drew up in his bull-nosed Morris. He wound down his window
and he grinned and said, "Leo Buchanan. You must be playing the
nurse." The nurse ...

Sadie Love at first sight then.

Margot No, it took a couple of weeks before I got the full blown
symptoms. He made me feel everything I wanted to be ... witty,
intelligent, beautiful.

Sadie Ah, the recognition...

Margot Yeah. He even said I had Botticelli feet. You wouldn't think
it, would you? Look at them.

Sadie This was during rehearsals?

Margot Yeah but we made a pact ... not to go the whole hog, you know — the full fandango until after the play had opened.

Sadie How romantic.

Margot We blew it of course.

Sadie The pact?

Margot In the interval on the first night ... In my dressing room. (*Laughing at the memory*) What a business with all the petticoats and tights and his codpiece and what-have-you.

Sadie He was always telling me what fun the two of you had together.

Margot Was he? Bless him. What about you?

Sadie I don't know — despite all my denials, I suppose he was a father figure really ... Quite sexy though.

Margot Especially after breakfast if I remember.

They both laugh

(Beat) Why did he have to come down here to die, for God's sake? I mean if he'd died anywhere else — Haywards Heath or Honolulu — I could have held on to the idea he didn't give a damn about me any more.

Sadie (*offering a Kleenex*) Your mascara has gone a bit ...

Margot Thank you. (*Wiping her eyes*) It's daft, isn't it? But the truth is a day hasn't gone by, not in all these years, when I haven't missed the bastard.

Sadie notices a bag by the window. She fetches it

Sadie Isn't this his bag? It's got something in it. It's rather heavy. Do you think we should hand it over?

Margot To hell with that.

Sadie (*taking out a parcel*) It's got your name on it.

Margot (*opening it*) What's this? (*Reading from a card*) "I would I were thy bird ..."

Sadie From the balcony scene.

Margot (*touched*) He was always a dreadful old ham.

They unwrap it

Sadie Oh, my God ... It's ...
Margot The Augustus John ... (*Somewhat taken aback*) Hold it up will you ... Oh, dear, oh, dear ... Look at me ... Look at me in my cornflower blue dress. Head in the air.
Sadie Leo was the anonymous buyer.
Margot So it seems. He paid eighty-five thousands pounds for it. (*Chuckling*) Daft old prune. He had to buy it off himself.
Sadie Why would he do that?
Margot Because he didn't want his wife to know. Poor lamb, he didn't have the *cojones* to tell her what he was doing. I don't think I've ever been so touched. The old bugger.

They hear Lady Buchanan approaching

Quick. Put it behind the curtain.

Sadie puts the picture behind the curtain

Lady Buchanan enters

Lady Buchanan Oh, good. You're still here.
Sadie I'm just going ...
Lady Buchanan It seems I owe you thanks and apologies, Sadie. You turned down Graham Latimer's offer?
Margot What offer?
Sadie He wanted me to kiss 'n' tell — "the marriage wrecker's story."
Lady Buchanan And you turned him down?
Sadie Yes.
Margot How much?
Lady Buchanan Fifty thousands pounds apparently.
Margot Are you mad?

Lady Buchanan You denied it. You told him there was no truth in the rumour about you and Leo. Why did you do that?

Sadie Does it matter? ... Perhaps I'm just not quite as trashy as you think.

Lady Buchanan Obviously not. Well, thank you. Thank you very much. I am sorry I was ... rude.

Sadie *It's OK ... Well, I'll just go and order a taxi. Goodbye, Lady* Buchanan.

Lady Buchanan Goodbye.

Sadie exits

I just came to say goodbye.

Margot I'm sorry I was rude too — as you said, cantankerous.

Lady Buchanan I was always terrified he'd leave me. And who could blame him? You see, I've always been a bit frightened of — you know — letting go. Even my father used to call me Little Miss Prickly. I am probably a very irritating woman.

Margot Well, we all can be.

Lady Buchanan Leo would have liked me to be a bit more bohemian. You know, leave the top off things and use packet soups. Lighten up, kind of thing. He was always going on about how funny you were. I couldn't bear it ... I've never been very amusing.

Margot studies this poor pathetic woman

Margot Maybe not but the point is — he loved you. He really did ... (*Inventing*) In fact that's why he came to see me.

Lady Buchanan I beg your pardon?

Margot Under the circumstances it would be too mean of me not to tell you. He said he'd got himself tangled up with a young girl. I didn't know then that it was Sadie, and he didn't know what to do.

Lady Buchanan That's why he came here?

Margot Yes. He said the thought of losing you was unbearable.

Lady Buchanan Really?

Margot He said he'd had enough of it all. (*Remembering*) ... In fact
he said all he really wanted was to be on a terrace in the South of
France, with the sun setting on the sea in front of him, and a great
wall of bougainvillea behind him. A glass of Pouilly Fuissé in his
hand and you beside him playing backgammon in a daft old hat.
Lady Buchanan Ah. I can just hear him saying it.
Margot He had a way with words.

Mrs Kidd enters

Mrs Kidd Your car's here, Lady Buchanan.
Lady Buchanan I'll be there in a minute.

Mrs Kidd goes

(*Picking the card out of the waste-paper basket*) You were wrong,
you know, about why I came to see you. I really did want to bury
the hatchet. (*Giving it to Margot*) You threw my birthday card in the
waste-paper basket. Please open it.
Margot (*opening it*) Lovely ... What's this?
Lady Buchanan A cheque for eighty-five thousand pounds. It's from
the sale of the Augustus John ...
Margot I'm speechless ...
Lady Buchanan Not you, surely. I felt so guilty. It was all my fault. I
forced Leo to sell it, you see.
Margot Did you?
Lady Buchanan Well, would you want a painting of your husband's
first wife on your sitting room wall?
Margot Perhaps in the downstairs loo.
Lady Buchanan This was the least I could do.
Margot I am very touched, Judy, and very grateful. Do you think I
should give you a kiss?
Lady Buchanan Why not?

They kiss

Margot I shall rather miss hating you.

Lady Buchanan Well, don't. There's no need. (*Moving to leave*) Leo's such a silly billy — he knows perfectly well I don't play backgammon ...

Lady Buchanan exits

Margot (*looking for a pen*) Pen ... pen. Here we are. (*She writes a cheque*)

Sadie enters

Sadie My cab is on its way.

Margot Good. You'll be very good as Juliet. You've got the happiness.

Sadie Have I? Not just now, I haven't.

Margot It'll come back — it's in your bones. Watch out for your Romeo and all that "palpable heat". (*Handing her the cheque*) Here, this is for you ... A present.

Sadie Eighty-five thousands pounds ... Are you crazy?

Margot Just a bit. It actually comes via Lady Buchanan. From the sale of the painting. What goes round ——

They kiss

Sadie — comes round. Thank you so much. What about you? Will you be ok?

Margot Oh, yes. I've got the painting to remind me of how young and daft I once was. Off you go.

Sadie exits

Alone Margot lifts up the picture

(*To the painting*) Happy birthday Me.

Curtain

FURNITURE AND PROPERTY LIST

SCENE 1

On stage: Table. *On it*: money box containing coins. Telephone
Chairs
Curtains (at window)
Waste-paper basket

Off stage: Newspaper (**Mrs Kidd**)
Card. *In it*: cheque (**Lady Buchanan**)
Bag. *In it*: parcel. *In it*: picture (**Sir Leo**)

Personal: **Margot**: mobile, coins
Freda: iPod, headphones
Sadie: notebook, pen
Sir Leo: mobile

SCENE 2

Set: Kleenexes
Used tissues (in waste-paper basket)
Brandy
Pen
Cheque

LIGHTING PLOT

Practical fittings required: nil
1 interior. The same scene throughout

To open: General interior lighting

No cues

EFFECTS PLOT

Printed by The Kingfisher Press, London NW10 7AS

Lightning Source UK Ltd.
Milton Keynes UK
UKHW021534080522
402613UK00008B/449